9-28-14

PLUMSTER BUNNY

Written by Craig Howard
Pictures by Nic The Artist & Lance Wheeler

Little Timmy had a big problem! For the first time in his life, he had to sleep in his own room. No longer could he sleep in his parents' room.

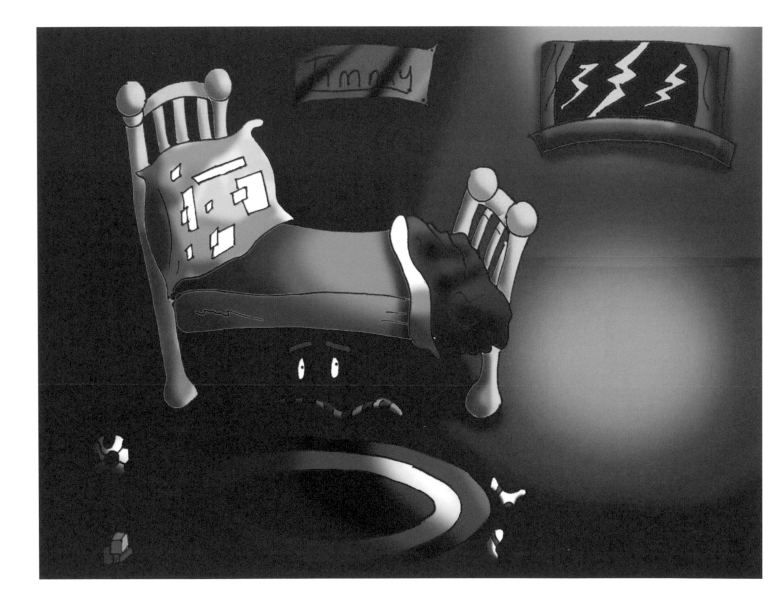

Man! Oh! Man! As Little Timmy hid under his bed, paralyzed with fear, he wished he had someone or something to stay in his room with him.

Then in a cloud of smoke,
appearing for the first time,
was PLUMSTER BUNNY!

Little Timmy let out a loud shriek.

"Hi Little Timmy. Don't be afraid. It's me PLUMSTER BUNNY. I'll stay here with you and be your friend."

Little Timmy took a step
forward and started to relax.
PLUMSTER BUNNY seemed to
be really cool. He and
PLUMSTER BUNNY talked
for a while and played a few
games. Little Timmy felt
really wonderful.

Little Timmy was worried about trying to go to sleep but he knew PLUMSTER BUNNY would protect him and stay by his side no matter what happened. Just as Little Timmy was telling PLUMSTER BUNNY that he was ready to rest, without warning out of the closet came a strange noise.
"RrRr! RrRr!"
Little Timmy and PLUMSTER BUNNY looked up. "Aggghhhh," screamed Little Timmy!

It was RrRr, THE SCARIEST MONSTER IN THE WORLD!!!! The more RrRr made the noise, the more terrified Little Timmy became. RrRr wouldn't stop or go away.

Little Timmy was very afraid. Then he heard **PLUMSTER BUNNY** whisper, "Never fear Little Timmy, I'm on your side."

With that, PLUMSTER BUNNY stepped forward shielding Little Timmy from the monster, and stared directly into RrRr's many eyes, very, very intently. He used THE PLUMSTER BUNNY STARE!!!!!!!

RrRr felt confused. His mind began to reflect on how horrible his behavior had been. Scaring children was wrong and he knew it. RrRr was ashamed and begged PLUMSTER BUNNY and Little Timmy for forgiveness. He pleaded to be friends with the two of them. He explained that he had no friends and that was why he had behaved so horribly.

PLUMSTER BUNNY and Little Timmy began to understand and smiled.

They were in agreement as Little Timmy said, "Certainly RrRr! Everyone makes mistakes but you can always fix things if you try hard enough to change."

After spending some
time playing with
PLUMSTER BUNNY and
RrRr, Little Timmy
started to get sleepy.

He yawned and said a sleepy goodnight to his new friends. Then, Little Timmy crawled into bed.

PLUMSTER BUNNY and RrRr pulled the covers up and tucked Little Timmy in. Before they knew it, he was fast asleep.

PLUMSTER BUNNY and RrRr sighed and smiled at each other. Both felt really fabulous about all the new friendships they formed. They waved goodbye and went on their merry way.

At an early age, Craig Howard learned that perseverance and understanding coupled with a strong education were essential tools when aspiring to lead a productive life. Though mathematics proved to be very challenging for Mr. Howard, it didn't prevent him from successfully thriving on Wall Street for approximately twenty years. Craig started at the American Stock Exchange and wrapped up his career at First New York Securities and Perceptive Capital Hedge Fund before retiring in 2006.

Mr. Howard is eager to share his vast knowledge and expertise with everyone who is willing to listen. In March 2011, the Plumster Bunny project was born. Through Plumster Bunny, Craig Howard hopes to spread positive CONFLICT RESOLUTION messages to young children. The Plumster Bunny motto is Friendship Building One Plum at a Time!!!

In addition, Mr. Craig Howard seeks to provide fresh clean water to areas deprived of such necessities. He strongly believes that one person can make an influential difference.

PLUMSTER BUNNY
(201) 208-3055
plumsterbunny@gmail.com
www.facebook.com/plumsterbunny.com

Picture coloring and book layout by
Nic The Artist
nictheartist@yahoo.com
THE ARTIST